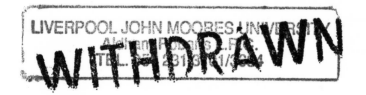

The Cradle Place

Also by Thomas Lux

The Cradle Place

Thomas Lux

HOUGHTON MIFFLIN COMPANY   BOSTON   NEW YORK   2004

For information about permission to reproduce selections from this book,
write to Permissions, Houghton Mifflin Company, 215 Park Avenue South,
New York, New York 10003.

Visit our Web site: www.houghtonmifflinbooks.com.

Library of Congress Cataloging-in-Publication Data

Lux, Thomas, date.
The cradle place / Thomas Lux
 p.   cm.
ISBN 0-618-42830-5
 I. Title.
PS3562.U87C73 2004
811'.54—dc22   2003067554

Book design by Melissa Lotfy

Printed in the United States of America

WOZ 10 9 8 7 6 5 4 3 2 1

Many of the poems in this book first appeared, sometimes in slightly different form, in
the following magazines:

American Poetry Review: *The Devil's Beef Tub; Debate Regarding the Permissibility of
Eating Mermaids; Burned Forests and Horses' Bones; Dry Bite; Can't Sleep the Clowns
Will Eat Me; Letter to Walt Whitman from a Soldier He Nursed in Armory Square
Hospital, Washington, D.C., 1866; Can Tie Shoes But Won't; Goofer-Dust; Terminal Lake;
Monkey Butter; Three Vials of Maggots; Render, Render; Portrait of X [III]; Remora.*
Atlantic Monthly: *The Gletz* (under the title *The Diamond Cutter*). Canary River: *With
Maeterlinck's Great Book.* 88: *Guide for the Perpetually Perplexed.* Field: *Uncle Dung
Beetle; Myope; To Help the Monkey Cross the River; Flies So Thick above the Corpses in
the Rubble, the Soldiers Must Use Flamethrowers to Pass Through.* Five Points: *Breakbone
Fever.* Greensboro Review: *Rather.* Gulf Coast: *Ten Years Hard Labor on a Guano Island;
Scorpions Everywhere.* Kenyon Review: *The Magma Chamber.* Lumina: *The Ice Worm's
Life.* MARGIE: *From the High Ground; To Plow and Plant the Seashore.* New Delta
Review: *Dystopia.* Passages North: *Reject What Confuses You.* Pedestal: *Thus, He Spoke
His Quietus; National Impalement Statistics.* Rialto (UK): *The Chief Attendant of the
Napkin; If One Can Be Seen.* San Diego Reader: *The Professor of Ants;* 174517: *Primo
Levi, an Elegy.* Willow Springs: *Birds Nailed to Trees; Boatloads of Mummies; The Late
Ambassadorial Light; Say You're Breathing.*

The American Fancy Rat and Mouse Association was first published by Fameorshame-
press as a limited-edition broadside.

Special thanks to Mary Cornish, Arjun Shetty, and Ginger Murchison.

for my blood: Elinor, my mother,
Norman, my father,
and Claudia, my daughter

Morn came and went—and came, and brought no day.

—BYRON

I want the old rage, the lash of primordial milk!

—THEODORE ROETHKE

Contents

The Cradle Place

I

The Late Ambassadorial Light

Light reaches through a leaf
and that light, diminished, passes through
another leaf,
and another, down
to the lawn beneath.
Green, green, the high grass shivers.
Water over a stone, and bees,
bees around the flowers, deep-tiered beds
of them, yellows and golds and reds.
Saw-blade ferns feather in the breeze.
And, just as a cloud's corner
catches the sun, a tiny glint in the garden—the milk
of a broken stalk? A lion's tooth?
Or might that be the delicate labia
of an orchid?

Say You're Breathing

just as you do every day, in and out, in and out, and in each
breath: one tick
of a shaving from a bat's eyelash, an invisible sliver
of a body mite
who lived near Caligula's shin, diamond dust (we each inhale a carat
in a lifetime), a speck of scurf
from the Third Dynasty (that of the abundant
imbeciles), one sulfurous grain
from the smoke of a mortar round, a mote of marrow
from a bone poking through a shallow grave,
a whiff from a mummy grinder
caught in a Sahara wind, most of the Sahara itself,
inhaled in Greenland, sweat dried to crystal on your father's lip
and lifted to the sky
before you were born—all, all, a galaxy
of fragments floating
around you every day,
inhaled every day,
happy to rest in your lungs
until they are dust again
and again risen.

Dry Bite

When the krait strikes but does not loose
his venom: dry bite. What makes the snake choose
not to kill you? Not *Please*,
not *I didn't mean*
to step on you. He may be fresh out: struck
recently something else. But: if he withholds
his poison,
when does he do so and why?
Can he tell you are harmless to him?
He can't swallow you, so why kill you?
There's no use asking the krait: he's deaf.
In that chemical, that split-billionth
of a second, he decides
and the little valve
of his venom sac
stays shut or opens wide.
Dry, oh dry, dry bite — lucky the day
you began to wear
the krait's snake-eyed mark
on your wrist
and you walked down the mountain
into the valley
of that which remains of your life.

Horse Bleeding to Death at Full Gallop

(La Florida, 1540)

Four arrows in him, wait, five,
one so deep its feathers lie
beneath his coat. His rider's dead,
fallen off, eleven arrows in his neck
between helmet and breastplate,
a bloody, spiky collar. Without the weight
of the rider, his lance, spurs, the horse still
runs, runs whip-blind, over the green hills
until he reaches the white-sand shore
and he can run or walk no more.

Debate Regarding the Permissibility
of Eating Mermaids

Cold-water mermaids, and only on Fridays, said Pope Ignace VII.
Sumerian texts suggest consent if human parts
predecease fishy parts,
but cuneiform detailing this
was lost to tomb robbers.
The British Admiralty, sixteenth century, deemed it anthropophagy
and forbade it,
though castaways, after sixty days,
were exempted
upon the depletion of sea biscuits. Taboo! Taboo!, said the South Sea
Islanders, though a man could marry one
if his aquatic skills
impressed her enough. Conversely, a woman, no matter
how well she swam,
could not marry with a merman. Uruguayans, Iowans,
leave no records on the subject.
The Germans find it distasteful,
though recently declassified World War II archives
suggest certain U-boat captains . . .
No problem for the French: flambéed or beneath béarnaise.
The official Chinese position is they don't have a position!
—But I grow weary of this dour study,
tired of the books
wherein this news is hidden, the creaking shelves
in museum basements, the crumbling pages
of the past and future, I'm tired
of this foggy research
to which I've devoted decades
trying to find the truth in these matters
and what matters in such truth.

The Professor of Ants

For his whole life ants were the life of the Professor of Ants. On his belly, on his hands, knees, above the world of ants: which colony forages where, when, what; which tribes cooperate with other tribes, which tribe attacks the smaller tribes. All day, the sun hammering his shoulders and neck above the world of ants. Some days he gives them shade they did not know before. He recognizes many by their marks or missing legs. The Professor's got his pen and clipboard out, season after field season. There go the leaf cutters, off to work, 6:45 A.M., to shear their sails of green. The harvesters carry tiny sacks of seeds to sow and little hoes to weed their rows of fungi. And, from a large colony, starting out on their thrice-yearly slave-making raids, the sanguine ants. When the sanguines are away—the Professor has noted, and twice published, this fact—sometimes a golden-haired beetle (*Hylurgus ligniperda*) moves into their nest, and when the sanguines return (carrying their slaves!) the beetle secretes a drink that makes the slavers her slaves, and the new slaves of the slavers her slaves as well. The sanguines need the slaves to groom their eggs. The beetle needs the ants to feed her and hers. The ants don't need the beetle at all. The Professor needs the ants to feed him and his. Back at the lab, at the chalkboard, he wishes not to feel what they feel with their feelers.

Tactile

One eyelash, one
millimeter
longer than each other eyelash on your left eyelid, bends
at its tip, as it, alone, leans
on my lowest left rib's ledge, this single filament
holding your bones
to mine. A touch of no touch, a touch
so light the tactile scale's
needle barely breathes. Then,
attached to a human as it is,
this one eyelash
lashes me there, many times,
and tonight the tiny scars shine
in the blue-stone dark.

Ten Years Hard Labor on a Guano Island,

said His Honor, handing you a pick
and a shovel
and a ticket
for a boat ride here
where the shovel is chained
to your right wrist
and to the left, a bucket.
The pick you'll wear strapped to your back
until it's time to pick with it.
You'll dig, for a decade, down
through the strata the seabirds left over eons
and, one by one, haul the bucketfuls
to the dockside piles.
The birds stopped here to rest awhile,
the roaming, the landless,
the long-distance birds on protracted wings.
On days, working the cliffs, when you can overlook
the sea, you might see—a foot
or two above the waves,
as you mine his ancestors' guts—you might still see one.

Family Photo Around Xmas Tree

Dad's left arm reaches across Mom's back
and even across Dottie's, his daughter's,
and just touches with his fingertips
his son Rusty's shoulder.
Dottie's ten, Rusty eight, though small for his age
and his left eye a little lazy.
The tree thick
with foil and lights, lit candles and a mantel hung
with monogrammed socks. Reindeer race
across Dad's sweater. If you lift
this picture to your nose, you smell cider
and snow, Mom's valley-of-the-lily
perfume. The fire's
pine knots snap. Oh bless this family
and their dog, Chocolate,
bless this house and hearth,
and bless Grammy, who will be here soon,
though Grandpa won't
this year, nor dear Aunt Elsie, dear, dear Aunt.
The big blue bowl of crabmeat salad she brought
each year ditto won't be here. Bless
this family, the living and the dead,
and may they never send a card
or newsletter to me again.

Rather

Rather strapped face to face with a corpse, rather an asp
forced down my throat, rather a glass
tube inserted in my urethra
and then member smashed
with a hammer, rather wander the malls of America shopping
for shoes, rather
be lunch, from the ankles down,
for a fish, rather mistake rabbit drops
for capers, or pearls, rather my father's bones crushed to dust
and blown — blinding me — in my eyes,
rather a flash flood of liquid mud,
boulders, branches, drowned dogs, tear through Boys Town
and grind up a thousand orphans, rather
finger puppets
with ice picks
probe me, rather numbness, rather Malaysian tongue worm, rather rue,
rather a starved rat
tied by his tail to my last tooth,
rather memory become mush,
rather no more books be written but on the sole subject of self, rather
a retinal tattoo, rather buckets of bad bacilli and nothing else
to drink, rather the blather
at an English Department meeting, rather
a mountain fall on my head than this,
what I put down here, rather
all of the above than this, this:_____.

Portrait of X [III]

Purblind, he rose, shot his cuffs, and hit
the door, a gangster
but gangless, dead in the heart, dead
in the rat-black rumdum redundant heart, lost
to this world and not RSVPing
invites to the next.
Is this the one who would lead us to a new aesthetic?
Is this the one, fragile, moribund, afraid,
who will lead the fragile, moribund, and afraid?
Is this the New Truth messenger,
the one who will define
the New Politics
or the New Poetics
with the Old Oblique?
His famous sneer eats his gut like a worm.

Three Vials of Maggots

were collected from the corpse
found lying in a field
near a small stream. From these the lab can tell
at what time the dead one died.
They have schedules, the flies.
Some lay eggs
which hatch to maggots
which consume the corpse. Others come to eat flies, maggots, eggs.
Hide beetles arrive to clean the gristle.
It's an orderly arrangement.
What the maggots do
they do for you.

Uncle Dung Beetle

Hail, Uncle Dung Beetle!, he who
wherever dung meets dirt, which is everywhere, is our sweet savior,
without whom
each of us on the planet up to our necks
in two-day-old—crusty on the outside,
soft in the middle—cow pies,
without whom
the gloomy stench
of earth everywhere infused gloomier,
without whom
the worms could not carry their burden alone,
without whom the earth
receives less nitrogen
and more bacteria eat their way through intestines,
without whom no breathtaking
specializations: the dung beetle who lives
in a sloth's rump fur and leaps off to ride
his host's droppings to the ground, a jarred
but instant claimant,
without whom
we would be swallowing shovelfuls of flies each day,
without whom
only in heaven
(and then only after all the dead are evicted!)
would it be possible to live.

The Gletz

Through the loupe or peepstone it's there: a mini-
dot of air,
and when light shines through
the object, the gletz is visible via microscope, x-ray scope.
It's a flaw, diminishing
an object: when light,
unimpeded,
passes through it
the object's brilliance
is most brilliant. A gletz affects
clarity, affects merit.
It's best if no gletz can be found at all.
The gletz's place matters: higher up, bad news;
lower, less-bad news.
They indicate fragility,
these breathless, cell-sized cells
where two inmates are locked
and each has a knife.

Can Tie Shoes but Won't,

—for Brendan Constantine

it said on his report card, five years old, the boy
so slung
against the river's current he was later lost
in his paper canoe, paddled
himself lost, or half lost, or less lost than most, not
in the midriver flotilla with all the other boats
fighting the main and churning current,
but instead along and beside and even under
the river's banks—the place of overhangs
and eddies, sloughs
and whirlpools, the shaded
place beneath the bug-brailled leaves,
the python-laden branches, the place
beneath the bank's cool clay, between the roots,
where the toothy creatures
cache their prey
for later. Did he travel always
on one side of the river? No.
How did he cross to the other side? Carefully,
cutting the current without fighting it,
giving up some distance to it, in order that,
just so,
the shade, the light, the slight un-
dulations of the river's bends, are changed,
with intention,
and for years, upstream, a lifetime,
this way, upstream he goes,
this way, upstream,
on his voyage.

The American Fancy Rat and Mouse Association

Rat breeders gather
to primp and parade their best—the chinchilla rat,
silks, the Moluccan cream belly—at this dog show
for mice and rats where, if entered a cat,
there would be no crowning
this year of Rat of the Year, Mouse of the Decade.
The judge cradles a quaking contestant in her palm.
Reputations made or broken, breeding secrets, build
a better cancer rat and your pride can turn to cash, pack
another gram of fat
on the thighs of a mouse
and this news shivers up and down the row
of herpetologists here for the show.
Then, in another, a back row,
sit those whose interests lie in mouse and rat aesthetics
rather than in their behavior
or market potential—Oh the beautiful,
beautiful rats, they sigh, oh the beautiful rats.

To Help the Monkey Cross the River,

which he must
cross, by swimming, for fruits and nuts,
to help him
I sit with my rifle on a platform
high in a tree, same side of the river
as the hungry monkey. How does this assist
him? When he swims for it
I look first upriver: predators move faster with
the current than against it.
If a crocodile is aimed from upriver to eat the monkey
and an anaconda from downriver burns
with the same ambition, I do
the math, algebra, angles, rate-of-monkey,
croc- and snake-speed, and if, *if*
it looks as though the anaconda or the croc
will reach the monkey
before he attains the river's far bank,
I raise my rifle and fire
one, two, three, even four times into the river
just behind the monkey
to hurry him up a little.
Shoot the snake, the crocodile?
They're just doing their jobs,
but the monkey, the monkey
has little hands like a child's,
and the smart ones, in a cage, can be taught to smile.

The Devil's Beef Tub

There are mysteries—why a duck's quack
doesn't echo anywhere
and: Does God exist?—which
will remain always *as* mysteries. So
the same with certain abstracts
aligned with sensory life: the tactile,
for example, of an iron bar
to the forehead. Murder
is abstract, an iron bar to the skull
is not. Oh lost
and from the wind not a single peep of grief!
One day you're walking down the street
and a man with a machete-shaped shard
of glass (its hilt
wrapped in a bloody towel) walks toward you,
purposefully, on a mission.
Do you stop to discuss hermeneutics with him?
Do you engage him in a discussion about Derrida?
Do you worry that Derrida might be the *cause* of his rage?
Every day is like this,
is a metaphor or a simile: like opening a can
of alphabet soup
and seeing nothing but X's, no, look
closer: little noodle
swastikas.

Boatloads of Mummies

embarked from Egypt to New Jersey in 1848.
Boatloads of mummies by sail
sold to a pulp mill
to make into paper.
Which venture (one tries to think
what the investors thought) didn't
work out: the stationery resulting
was gray
and gritty
and held not the black depths of ink.
One wonders where the remaining mummies went.
A few were ground to powder
and put in jars, and then on shelves of remedies,
but all the rest, three or four holdfuls,
where did they go
when the vision of capital failed
(as visions do, more often
than they don't), where did
the remaining mummified go?

Thus, He Spoke His Quietus,

—for Larry Levis (1946–1996)

Larry did, with his book *Elegy*, his elegy, his last
long rolling lines of sadness, of unsobbed sobs,
of his immense wrecked heart,
his finishing stroke,
his last hard dig
of the paddle before lifting it
from the water, and his canoe, on the silent straight line
cut by its keel,
beaches itself
on the sandy, the lighted, the silt-lapped, the other, shore.

The Magma Chamber

Here it boils and begins to build, deep in the core,
what will be lava, molten
rock, in great domed cathedrals of rage underground
eventually expelled—to air,
and land. Sometimes
the magma—feeding up into the spreading rift
to fill the cracks
between the separating plates—heals. Sometimes
it needs a way out
and finds it—bang!—and slow, remorseless rivers
of liquid rock, red rivers
of rock, find their way
to the sea—through houses and horses,
over beet fields and putting greens, over hospitals, eating
through, with fire,
anything that wants to stay in its place
and just go on being. The orb
is hot inside, hurt,
which is bad for those who gauge
and receive its rage.
Nothing can stop it
but the sea
which boils where it enters, nothing
but the sea is vast and deep
and cold enough
to take all this poured fury, nothing
but the sea (if it so pleases)
can make a new island, new mountains,
a new republic of hope.

Birds Nailed to Trees

So the birds, through
their bony yellow toes, are tacked
to branches
and look as if they chirp, and chirp well, indeed.
A bird on the ground
tugs a worm from its hole, a metaphor
for industry and joy. Her plump tail tilts
to the task. The worm holds on
by a hook in its gut.
There's a nest in the tableau too,
and three eggs, pastel blue
and glued
together. Mother, mother bird, on nest's edge,
huffs her belly feathers
and prepares to sit upon her hollow eggs.
A red bird curves
overhead, his dive halted—though perpetual—by one
wing pinned to a leaf
and a wire
strung from his beak
to the black corners of this box
of birds, *Our friends who fly,*
as they live today in your backyard.
And lookit over there: a cat smacking his eyes.
And the boy by the barn pumping his pellet gun hard.

II
(other voices)

Guide for the Perpetually Perplexed

Don't hurt your brain on this: if the arrow points left,
it's left you should go. Then
take your first right,
then the next right,
again the next right, then another
right. If you head-on a cement truck,
it is as it should be. Too much
perplexity and soon everyone's head
is a revolving hologram of a question mark!
Instead: if the sign says USE YOUR WORDS,
then use your words,
in this order: subject, verb, object.
Instead: if the sign says SHUT THE FUCK UP,
then you should shut the fuck up.
If it comes over the intercom to get in line,
for gosh sakes, then get in line, your wingbones
to the wall and eyes forward.
Do nothing to further perplex the other perplexed.
We'll let you know when it's single file for lunch,
where it's first your placemats of puzzles
and impossible dots to disconnect
followed by your beans, and your brown meat, gray,
over which you'll pray, oh yes, you'll pray,
if you don't want us to break your neck.

If One Can Be Seen

If one can be seen, how can one see?,
the One Afraid to Be Seen said
in my office
on a late February afternoon.
The gold seals on my diplomas leached
to yellow in the weak
light. I loathe Februarys.
The One Afraid to Be Seen
wore a puppet theater on his head.
I tried to answer his question.
Looking outward
while being looked at
need not stop you from going forth
into the world, I offered.
There was a cord
that the One Afraid to Be Seen
could pull to open the curtains on his face.
He moved as if to pull the cord
but didn't, then again
reached for it
and opened the curtains a shiver, then closed them again,
and again raised a hand as if
to open . . . and I whack-smacked
the puppet theater off his head
with a long, looping, knuckle-dusted backhand slap
I learned in not one of the best schools (but not a bad
one either) in my profession
and its appointed tasks.

The Year the Locust Hath Eaten

They chewed my lawn down to sand
and then polished
each facet of each sand grain
with their relentless wings and then
were up and off again, a huge ball,
a tornado, a rack-clacking
wind of them.
They ate the sheep of all but their wool.
They ate the trees' leaves, then the twigs, then the branches,
then the trunks,
then sent out sappers
for the roots. They gnawed fence posts
leaving parallel rows
of barbed wire
across bald fields.
They took down the haystacks
and found no needles.
They left the bookmobile
tireless and with but one book uneaten: (insert odious book
of your choice).
They consumed the letters in the attic,
all the letters from sea to land
and land to sea,
all the letters of funeral and woo.
Grandma's wedding dress—leaving a wreck
of pearl buttons—they devoured.
They buzz-cut the attic
and its sawdust sifted down
to the second floor—which was when I fled
and left behind the bitten land and the year
the locust hath eaten.

Burned Forests and Horses' Bones

are all we see when we cross the river
to this land. Two or three days, we guess, since the fire
reached this shore
and went to sleep.
This is where it stopped,
not where it started.
Why didn't it leap this narrow river?
We see but wisps, locally, of smoke.
We can't go back the way we came.
Before we crossed
to this scorched shore, we knew: we can't
go back whence we came.
The trail is charred with drifts of ash,
but passable. We are nine men, three women, seven children,
three mules—two pulling carts; the third, a pack
on its back—one dog, one duck.
We see nothing
but the burned bones
of horses, not for miles, nothing not gray or black.
Because his whiteness (though going
a grimy gray) offends us, we'll eat the duck.
Three more days we travel amid smoldering stumps,
crossing sooty streams, no sounds but the screech
our feet make on the black
and squeaky ground.
At night there is no wood with which to build a cooking fire.
Tomorrow we'll hack up an armoire
and kill and roast the dog.
Not one of the children will cry.

We have three mules yet, two carts.
We have one mission: to arrive
where the fire started
and pass over it to the place before the fire began.

Letter to Walt Whitman from a Soldier
He Nursed in Armory Square Hospital,
Washington, D.C., 1866

dear Walt, kind uncle, its near two years since I left Armory Sq.
& I'm home now. The corn grew good this summer and we
bought 2 cows. My leg ain't right still but it's still my leg. When
you prommiced they wouldn't take it was the first time after the
grapeshot I didn't want to go to the world where there is no
parting. Dear Uncle, we have had a son borned & we call him
Walter Whitman Willis, he is well & Bright as a dollar. Yrs
Affectionately, Bill Willis

Scorpions Everywhere

There goes one disguised as a mouse!
And those gray fellows, bushy tails,
who jump from tree to roof to fence.
Watch their eyes as they watch you
while they eat their nuts. They
are everywhere now
and, too, their cousins, the white-tailed browsers (Bambi
is a baby of their species' name) who eat
our suburb's shrubs and herbs;
and those that purr,
and those mouth-breathers, drooling woofers,
and the ones with bandit eyes who trash
the trash—all
of these creatures (and, too, their spawn) are not
as they seem.
Do not more and more of them move closer and closer?
Do you look out the window and see two?
Do you turn away, turn back, see three?
Do you hear the little brother of the wolf
howling from the marsh near the golf
course, the 8th tee? He
leads them all, quick, cunning, and assisted
by his minister, a gnat.
Each is, in fact—this is *certain*—a scorpion
and holds a phial of venom
until the time it's time to inject in you!
Ohhhh—on the day the wind is wrecked,
on the day the sky breaks,
on the day the sea creeps under a rock!

Myope

The boy can't see but what's right in front of him.
Ask him about that clock
across the room, he can't see it, or he don't
care. He makes a picture of a mountain—he's looking
at the mountain!—and it comes out fuzzy
and he puts in cliffs and fizzers
that ain't there. Sit an apple down
on the table and he can draw it in pencil, in color, once so right
I almost took a bite.
And he's got a nose on him like a hound.
His daddy says he can sniff a rat in a freezer.
A set of ears, too: he says he hears
his baby brother crying
and I can get to him
just as he opens his mouth to wail
and in my arms it's right to sleep again.
That comes in handy, sometimes. Sometimes
a baby's got to cry.
The boy's a bit odd.
He likes books a lot.
On a hot summer evening,
I swear, he's reading on the porch
and the turning pages make a breeze.

III

To Plow and Plant the Seashore

His tractor rattles down the dunes: low tide, it's time to plow
the seashore and then follow
with the finer harrow
blades to comb
this rich earth smoother. The bits of shell and weed
will contribute to the harvest.
He's not been farming long—see: he has all his fingers
to their tips. No, he's not been farming
long. Now his field is ready
and it's time to plant his seeds
in earth through which he pulled his farmer's tools.
This year, it's corn: he loves the little yellow crowns.
Yes, this year it's corn, the farmer thinks,
last year the soybeans didn't take
and the yield was: minus-beans, i.e., the seed beans, too, were gone.
Corn will love this rich and muddy ground
and grow in rows over his long but thin two acres.
That's what they gave the farmer: two acres, a tractor
with its partners,
and that little house
in the blue-green sea grass
above his field. Also four chickens.
They gave him four chickens
and a hammer, and a pitchfork.
This is what they gave him
and he was glad for it, and for his title: farmer.
His fields are tilled.
Someday he'll have a daughter and a son.
By morning, the farmer thinks, the shoots
will be up an inch or two.
The wronged one is always the wrong one.

Amphribrach Dance

Remember, first falling, and falling,
from lofty, from distant, from dizzy
cliff's slim ledge, yes falling, through clear, not
blue-burned air, yet falling, still falling
to soft sand, to hard sea, to longing
for longing, and much less: the broken,
the thunky, the dancing we each did,
the heels down, then toes up, then heels down,
the rocking, the forward and, yes, back—
its measure so awkward, the sad dance
we each did, remember, remember?

Remora

Clinging to the shark
is a sucker shark,
attached to which
and feeding off its crumbs
is one still tinier,
inch or two,
and on top of that one,
one the size of a nick of gauze;
smaller and smaller
(moron, idiot, imbecile, nincompoop)
until on top of that
is the last, a microdot sucker shark,
a filament's tip—with a heartbeat—sliced off,
and the great sea
all around feeding
his host and thus him.
He's too small
to be eaten himself
(though some things swim
with open mouths) so
he just rides along in the blue current,
the invisible point of the pyramid,
the top beneath all else.

National Impalement Statistics

One out of eight deaths occurring in the home
or on picnics
is impalement-related. Four
thousand and eleven people die
in home accidents in the USA each year (on average
over the past decade), so
that means 501.375 people die
of home impalements each year.
Two hundred and eighty-seven people die on picnics
each year in the USA, therefore 35.875 (one does not
round off human beings!) people die
by impalement
on picnics, mostly by fork, but many more than one might expect
by toothpick, particularly
in the Northeast region of the country.
The denotative: sharp object
enters one part of body
and, sometimes, emerges from another part of body, often,
though not always, ending in expiration.
One loves
the exceptions: he who lives with the shaft of a golf club
skewering his neck
and learns to walk sideways through doors; she who lives
with a long sliver of ice, ever unmelting,
in her chest . . . The home
is a bruised and burning place
and in it lives a worm,
and the picnic, the picnic
is eating on the ground
as leopards do
when they are not eating in the trees.

Asafetida

The good, good thing for you
as prescribed by another, bitter
to the taste,
and, too, it stinks
like a neck after a boot heel is lifted,
for a moment, from it.
Like an eely
spike in a sinus. A horse-choking pill
put in a plunger
and shot down your throat—it's *good*
for you, will improve you, you need it,
put a little honey on this tiny bomb
and take it down, take
it right down.

174517: Primo Levi, an Elegy

—for Michael Ryan

I thought Jews were just another denomination: Episcopalians, Methodists, Jews, Catholics, Lutherans, etc. I knew Hitler hated Jews. I know I hated Hitler. I was a child. The name of our parish was St. Philip's. I had no idea who St. Philip was. In confirmation class I was asked the name of a Jewish cleric and I said "a rabbit." I liked to play with words. I liked to read words. I liked the sound of words. In novels and poems and history books: I liked to read sentences. I read and read. I did other things too. But I read hundreds and hundreds of books. Many years passed. One day, my friend said to me: You should read this book. He read a lot of books too. He said he and his wife were reading your book aloud to each other every night. They lived deep in the country, in a farmhouse on a red hill. They were very broke during those years. Reading your book *aloud* to each other. When they finally got a little money they moved, and my friend said he felt compelled, as they were leaving the house for the last time, to open the cabinet beneath the kitchen sink. Wrapped around the drainpipe was a long, thick, gray snake trying to warm himself. I read your book and I read it aloud too, in my own lonely house — I read it for myself, for my friends, and for that snake, and this is why I'm writing to you now, though you no longer have an address, to tell you: I read your book. I *read* your book.

Goofer-Dust

(dirt stolen from an infant's grave around midnight)

Do not try to take it from my child's grave, nor
from the grave
of my childhood,
nor from any infant's grave I guard—voodoo, juju, boo-hoo rites
calling for it or not! This dust, this dirt, will not
be taken at dawn or noon
or at the dusky time,
and if you approach
this sacred place near midnight,
then I will chop,
one by one, your fingers off
with which you do your harm. Goofer-dust: if you want it,
if you need it, then
erect downwind from a baby's grave
a fine-meshed net
and gather it
one-half grain, a flaky mote, an infinitesimally small fleck
of a flake at a time
and in such a way
it is given to you
by the day, the wind, the world,
it is *given* to you, thereby
diminishing the need to steal
this dirt displaced by a child
in a child's grave.

With Maeterlinck's Great Book,

The Life of the Bee, I beheaded a bee
staggering on the glass
patio door as I opened it
to read above book
on above patio. The bee sluggish, first cold
coming on. I angled and aimed
the book's spine
to detach its head,
and did so. I had fifty or so more pages
to read. I was indifferent
to irony's blue acid bath: I don't get lost in
one-hundred-year-old books
about bees every day.
All I felt
was a desire to shake the hand of Maurice Maeterlinck,
who loved these creatures
and showed it so
in the choice and order of his words.

Terminal Lake

Although they know no other waters
and have no creation myths,
the fish don't like it here: no way out,
no river to swim upstream or down.
Terminal Lake squats there,
its belly filled by springs, rain
and ice and snow. It's deep,
Terminal Lake, and no one's gone to the bottom
and come back up.
All's blind down there, and cold.
From above, it's a huge black coin,
it's as if the real lake is drained
and this lake *is* the drain: gaping, language-
less, suck- and sinkhole.

The Chief Attendant of the Napkin

stands beside the king
when he dines,
a napkin hung
on his arm. It was his father's job,
and his father's father's. He stands to the right
so he can step forward
and turn to offer the king
his arm, a napkin rack,
from which the king removes the napkin,
dabs his mouth,
and returns it to its rack.
The king is a good king,
and his manners likewise.
Then he dies.
The new king is a bad king,
so the serfs cut off his hands.
He's a better king for it.
The Chief Attendant of the Napkin's task now?
Not only to attend the napkin
but also to dab the king's mouth.
His son will have this job.
It's better than the new
positions: the Chief Attendants of the Knife, the Fork,
and the Spoon. They
stand to the king's left
and two feet back so that the king
may call them singly
to the table, or, most often

in that common duo,
Knife and Fork. Spoon, poor Spoon
the king calls up front, alone,
for milk-sopped bread or gruely soup.

The Mountains in the River
on the Way to the Sea

Once, there were more mountains, bigger mountains.
The still-here mountains were bigger.
The Himalayas were four times bigger!
Then the rains came,
and the Jovian Winds,
and cold to crack the rain,
and they took some of the mountains every day
to the rivers, which took them,
a grain at a time, to the ocean.
Rain, wind, rivers: they do all the work
while the ocean waits
with its mouth open
at the river's mouth.
Just as the seas once rose to the mountains,
the mountains will go again
to the eternal sea's soft bed.

Reject What Confuses You

Reject what confuses you,
Outlaw what seduces you,
What did not spring from a pure will,
Into the flames with what threatens you.
   —firesong for Nazi book burnings

Most of us who most of the time wouldn't be shocked
would be
if you showed us the pictures in this book,
would be
horrified and prefer not to look
and be adamant our children not look
but also be tolerant—cornerstone
for us—and admit that the artist
can express herself however she wants,
First Amendment, free speech . . . But when reminded
we are paying
the artist, even meagerly, indirectly (taxes: NEA), then
we think otherwise: "I am commissioning
you, am in fact your collaborator, so don't
say (paint, photograph) that; I wouldn't." —Sorry,
I beg to differ, *au*
contraire! Don't give money
to support the arts, taxes or otherwise.
And (easy for some to say) don't take any money
before you make the art.
Ask them to pay after
you give them the art,
not before.

Flies So Thick above the Corpses in the Rubble, the Soldiers Must Use Flamethrowers to Pass Through

And the little roasted flies
fall into the ruins too,
and more flies come—shoo fly, shoo—
until there's nothing for them to come to
anymore, nothing but sky, blankety-blank blank *blank* sky.

The Ice Worm's Life

is sun-avoiding, and by burred flanks
they wriggle through the glacier
which they'll never leave
nor ever meet ice worms of a neighboring glacier.
To them is the unexamined life
worth living? By day
a few yards in/under ice
and then wild nights, wild nights
on the glacier's surface
where to them the wind brings pollen, fern spores,
and the algae
that tint the blue frozen water red. The ice worms gorge,
they gorge, thousands of them,
in the dark, in the cold, aspiring to grow
from one-tenth of an inch
to four-tenths of an inch.
All night, the glacier a lawn
of them bent by the wind, and by dawn
they've gone down into the ice to sleep,
to mate, until it is time
to ascend again: our refrigerative
fellow creatures, our neighbors
on the glacier beside ours
who, if we could invite them into our living rooms,
would decompose
in fifteen minutes (that soon!)
and go wherever their theology tells them they must go.

Provincia Aurifera

Let's go there: the gold-bearing land.
It's in the trees, beaches of it, it's sand!
You pick it up and put it in your pocket.
Let's go there: the gold-bearing land.
Look at your girl in the locket
she gave you: gold will be in your hands.
Let's go there: the gold-bearing lands,
it's in the trees, beaches of it, it's sand!

I Will Please, Said the Placebo

One hundred men have an inexplicable, harmless, numb
though painful space, or globule, or vacuum,
no bigger than a baby pea, smack
in the middle of their brains: an anti-tumor,
less than benign,
since there is no place
in which a malignancy may grow.
All these men are brought to a hospital,
lined up, and counted off: fifty odd,
fifty even. Then the doctors
give the experimental dose to the odds
and sugar pills to the evens.
They all go home, have dinner,
and take their pills. The doctors said: On top
of a full belly, take your pills. By morning,
fifty of the men had died,
peacefully, in sweet sleep, in greeny dreams.
Fifty still lived: twenty-five who took the sugar pill,
twenty-five who took the drug.
Autopsies and CAT scans
on the dead and the living, respectively,
showed no change
in the size of the emptiness, with one
exception: a tall, reedy
man, one of the dead,
whose anomaly
had shrunk, the doctors said,
to the size of a BB.

Hospitality and Revenge

You invite your neighbor over
for a beer and a piece of pie.
He says words inappropriate
about your Xmas bric-a-brac.
You shoot him, three times, in the face.
While you complain to his first son
re high off-white-couch cleaning costs,
he shoots you in the face five times.
At your wake, your first son pumps eight
slugs behind his first son's left ear.
Your wife invites your neighbor's widow for tea.

From the High Ground,

it's a grand view of valley and farm,
a lucid view of steeples and graveyards,
of all the tiny people up Main Street and down
Maple, of the middle and grammar schools too.
From the high ground's elevation: a long
look at the good boys and bad, a lengthy look
at the girl on the swing
as her skirt billows.
There's the mailman who reads every letter.
There's the ring in its box on a little black pillow.
There's the milkman taking too long to deliver his milk.
There's the librarian's undies on the line—silk.
From the high ground all is clear,
interpretable, luculent: *this* is what this *means*.
The Berchtesgaden view, a dog at your heel.
From the high ground (low shrubs
stubbed by thin winds)
the stony path reaches
higher still, loftier, to heaven almost,
as it grows narrower,
and more narrow.

Dystopia

For shoes: rat skins duct-taped around a foot.
Shirts: sacks used to haul corn
to High Feast Day dinners.
The same corn's husks
used to polish the boots of the adjutants
and baked into bread by the adjutants' adjutants.
There are no ribs without elbows in them.
There is no shoulder without the breath of another on it.
Coughing carries across seas and sod.
The Dysentery Ward fights the Typhus Ward
for a melon rind which, in the confusion,
is stolen by a leper
who silences his bell's clapper
with his thumb's stub.
When two love
here, and sometimes two do love here,
they are famished for each other
but too weak to rise from their pallets of straw
to kiss. It is by their serene looks
and one-eighth smiles
the grave crews
honor them—placing one first, the other second,
in a twenty-person trench.
No casseroles for the mourners.
The three or four remaining haves
are quickly eaten by the have-nots.

Monkey Butter

Monkey butter's tasty, tasty,
you put it in cookies and pie,
you mix it in cake, I can't tell you a lie:
don't be light with it, nor hasty
to push it aside. It's not too sweet,
with a light banana-y hue,
the monkeys all love it,
and so will the one you call *you*,
the *you* who's another you want to love you.
Put it in his pudding, in her pastry puff,
then sweep the table of all that other stuff.
Later, leave a little in his left, her right, shoe.

Breakbone Fever

On the femur a brick drops hard, from the top rib
to bottom a steel
bar slams, on neck bones and skull, on clavicle, the fever
drops its stones, on the knuckles,
the wrist bone; the carpals, both regular and meta-, they get
cellar doors slammed on them. Oh the capitate, hamate,
lunate, and pisiform bones take a bad
beating: ball-peens bang
and jackhammers
jack against each one. Even some joints—interphalangeal
agony!—ligaments, get this fever, go down
with it; even fingernails, nerveless themselves, battered by it,
and hair, hair enters the skull like a hot needle. Watch
out, ossicular chain—hammer, anvil,
stirrup, bones smaller than grains of rice
in the ear's pea-sized cave,
full grown since birth, first to turn
to ash, watch out—the pain there
will tell you who owns the heat,
who aligns the tenses—past, present, future, and none,
will show you who owns the fishhook frictive verbs,
who assigns the persons, places, and things,
who islands the ocean, who affords the tree its rings,
who owns, in fact, your blistering bones.

Can't Sleep the Clowns Will Eat Me

—for Claudia

it says on the dead
author's ("the author is dead") daughter's
T-shirt. He sympathizes with this line
and his daughter who wears it,
and recognizes that *its* author (who also
must be dead) wrote the line to describe
and mock dread, insomnia, fear.
The author, her father (continuing to be dead), buys
the shirt for his above-mentioned child
because she *likes* the line.
The author (dead as a brick) is glad
his daughter enjoys and understands
the line, that it's funny, parodic, odd.
This pleases the author (a rotting corpse)
and—forever, down the boulevard of elms and ash,
forever beside the indeterminate river into the long night,
forever with his child and their blood-on-blood—he will,
he will be happy
learning to live with being dead.

Render, Render

Boil it down: feet, skin, gristle,
bones, vertebrae, heart muscle, boil
it down, skim, and boil
again, dreams, history, add them and boil
again, boil and skim
in closed cauldrons, boil your horse, his hooves,
the runned-over dog you loved, the girl
by the pencil sharpener
who looked at you, looked away,
boil that for hours, render it
down, take more from the top as more settles to the bottom,
the heavier, the denser, throw in ache
and sperm, and a bead
of sweat that slid from your armpit to your waist
as you sat stiff-backed before a test, turn up
the fire, boil and skim, boil
some more, add a fever
and the virus that blinded an eye, now's the time
to add guilt and fear, throw
logs on the fire, coal, gasoline, throw
two goldfish in the pot (their swim bladders
used for "clearing"), boil and boil, render
it down and distill,
concentrate
that for which there is *no*
other use at all, boil it down, down,
then stir it with rosewater, that
which is now one dense, fatty, scented red essence

which you smear on your lips
and go forth
to plant as many kisses upon the world
as the world can bear!